Love to sit and relax? Love to color? This is the book for you. Unlike most adult coloring books you can buy these days this one is special because all the images are hand drawn. I started using my drawings as coloring pages while working for an inpatient psychiatric unit. The images were shared among the staff and clients as a source of entertainment. As humans I believe we are all connected and sharing my drawings with others to color is one of the many ways I try to connect with the world.

This book is a collection of drawings that I like to call abstracts. They aren't really anything at all, just lines on pages. For me the process is always intuitive and meditative. However the drawings have been inspired by the mhendi designs of India and western Asia I learned as a young girl as well as some zentangle patterns I've picked up or created on my own.

Remember to take time for yourself. Take time to breathe, take time to relax, and always take time to play.

As always, I try to approach every day with gratitude, so I would like to dedicate this page as a very warm thank you to all the friends and family who supported me by purchasing my first book. Thank you.

Thank you to my friends Santi and Larry for all the technical help.

To the owner of this book, a thank you to you as well. May you find time each day to be grateful and may this book bring you satisfaction. I encourage you to use the empty spaces to write, or draw, or just be creative.

Love and Gratitude.

Follow us on Facebook; Coloring with Friends

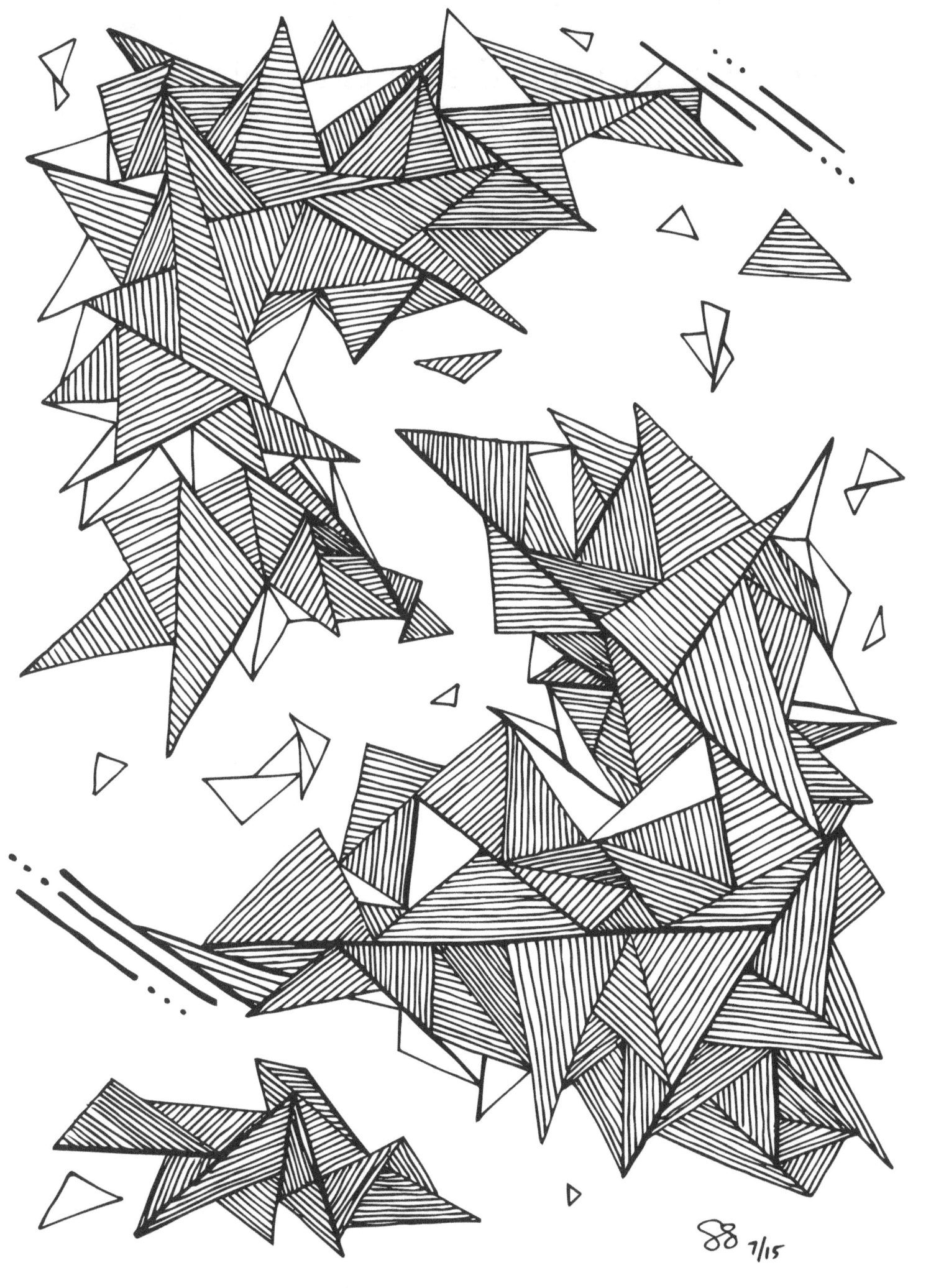

Procrastination is the art of keeping up with
yesterday.
~Don Marquis

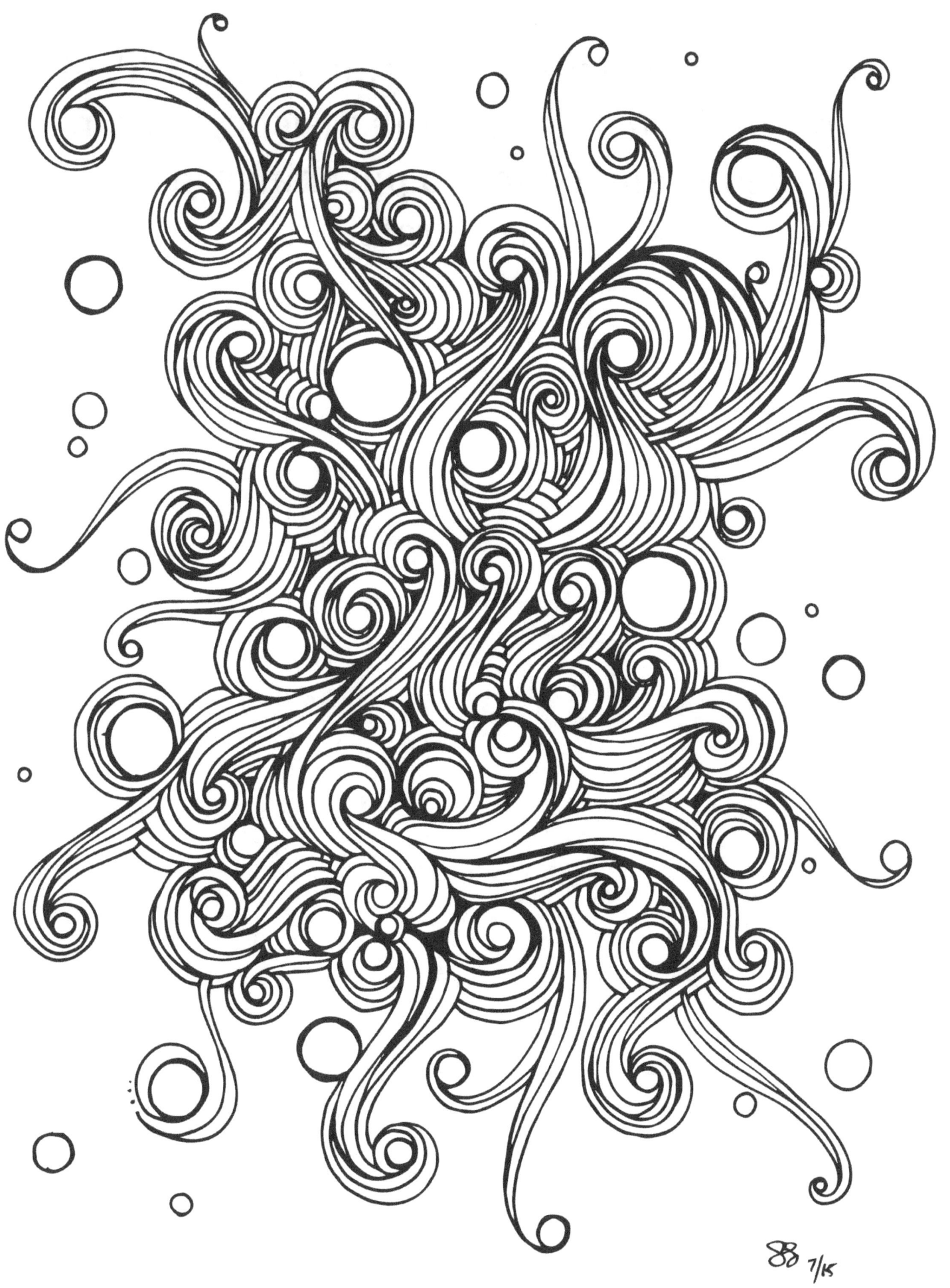

The trouble with having an open mind, of course, is that people will insist on coming along and trying to put things in it.
~Terry Pratchett

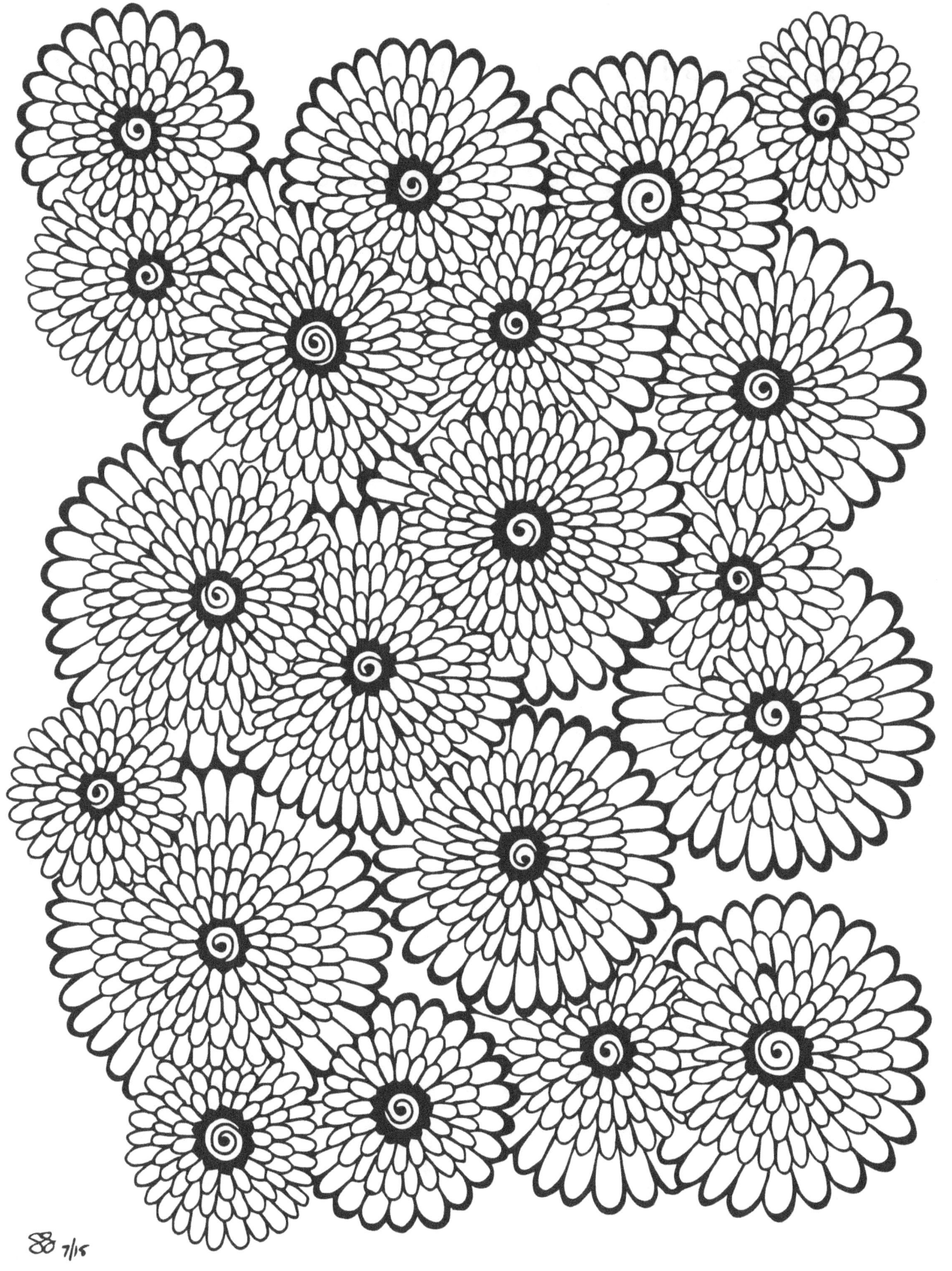

An idea isn't responsible for the people who believe in it.
~Don Marquis

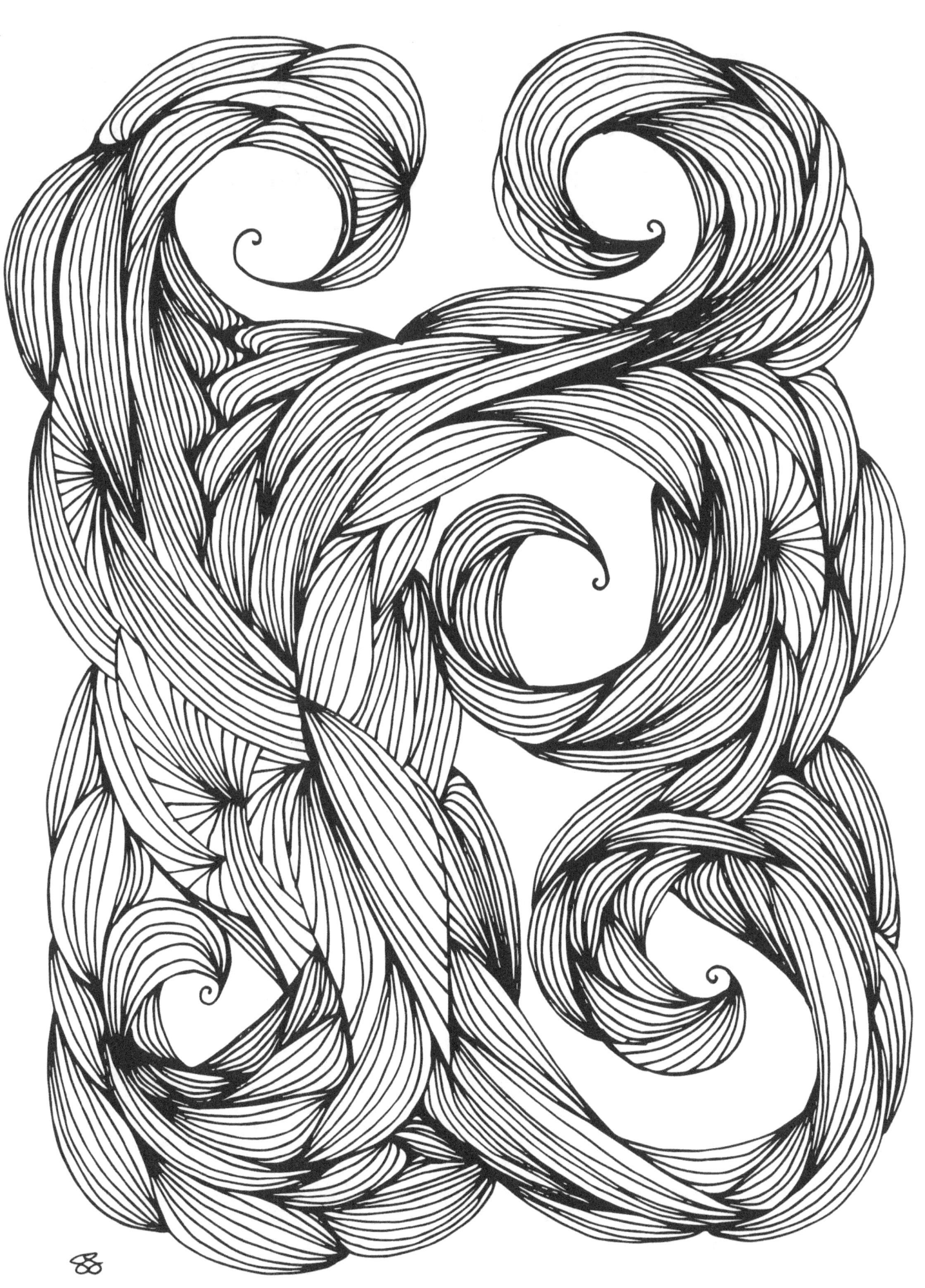

If you could kick the person in the pants responsible for most of your trouble, you wouldn't sit for a month.
~Theodore Roosevelt

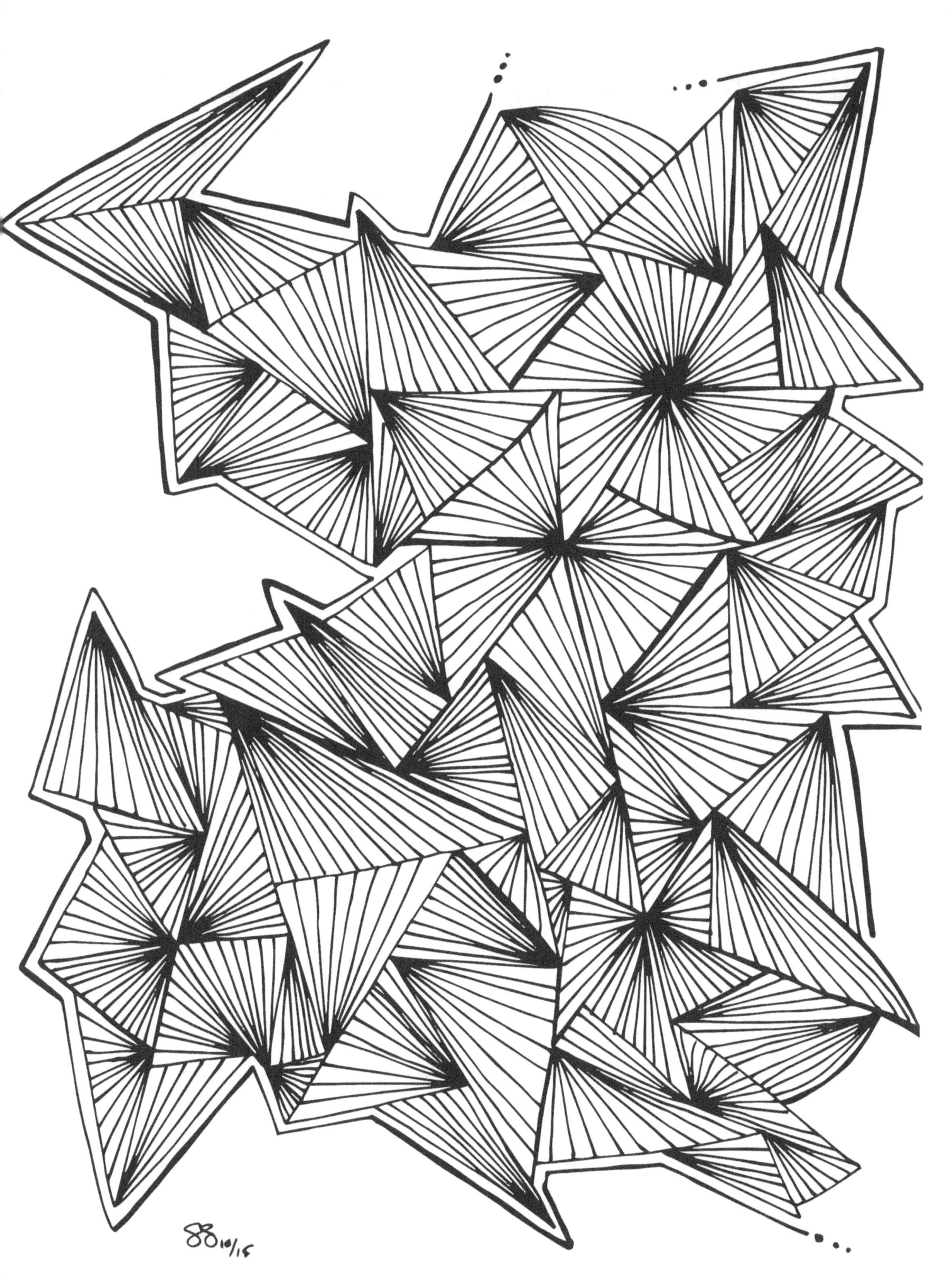

By all means let's be open-minded, but not so open-minded that our brains drop out.
~Richard Dawkins

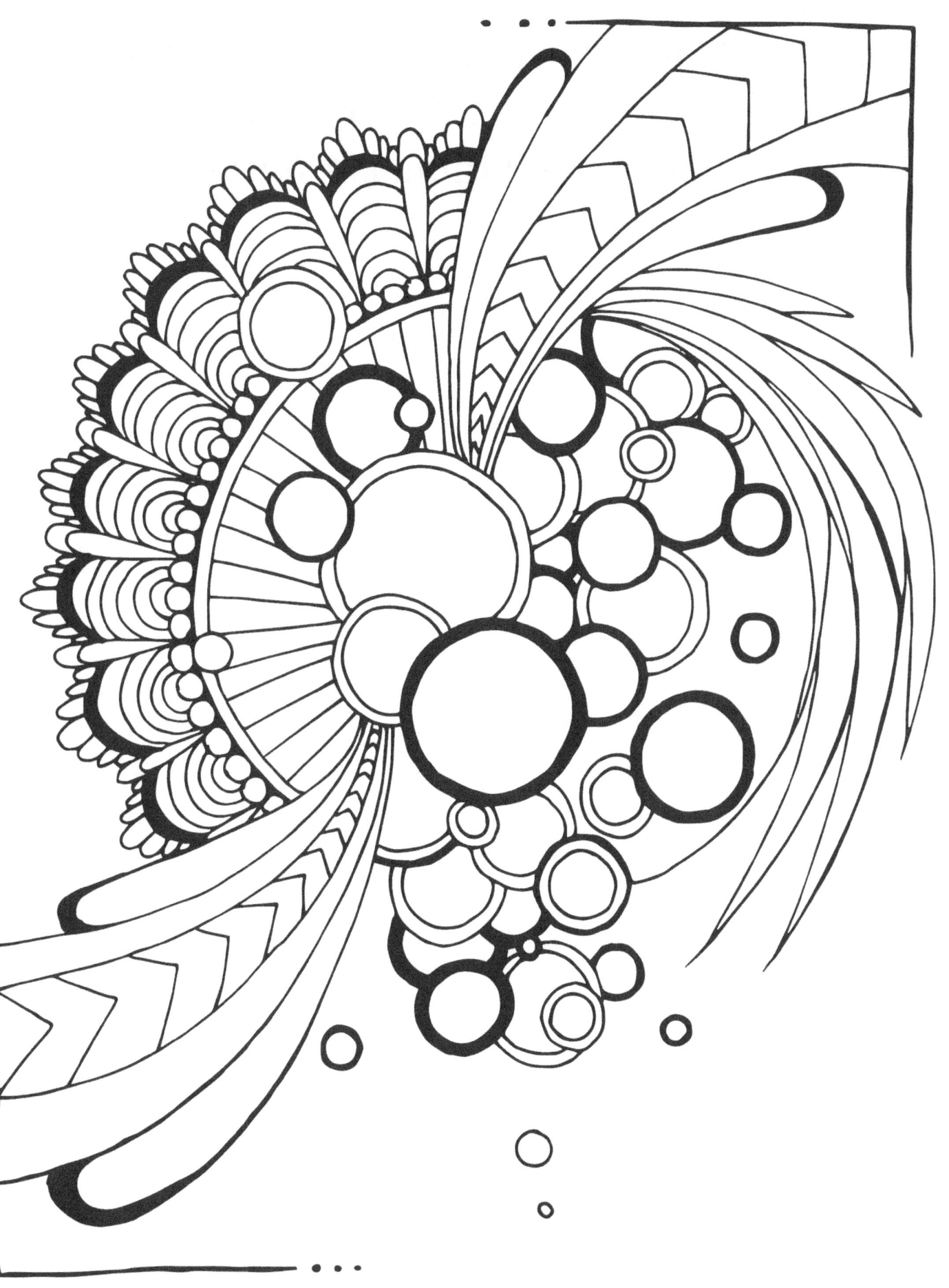

There are only two ways to live your life. One is as though nothing is a miracle. The other is as though everything is a miracle.
~Albert Einstein

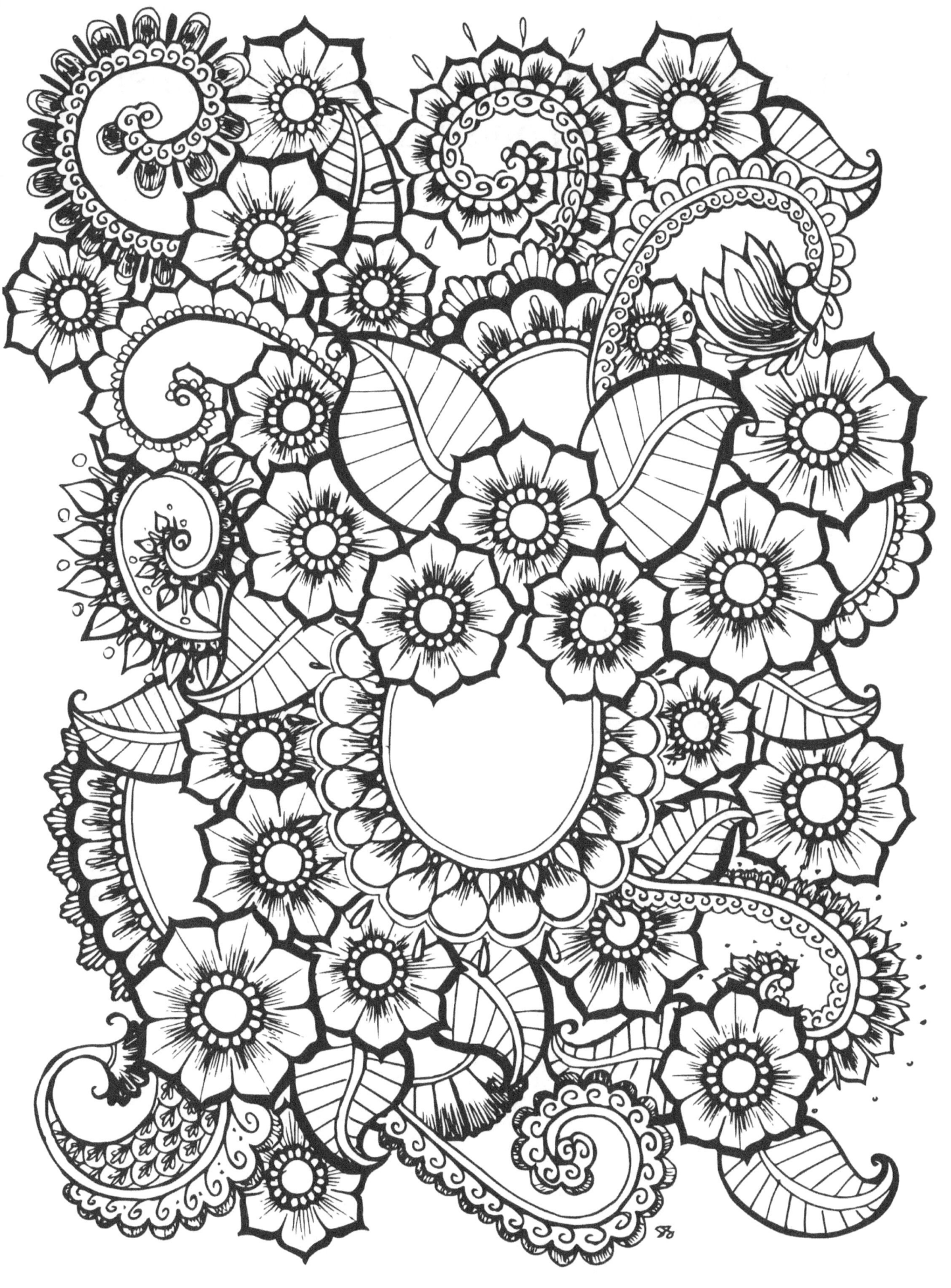

What is forgiven is usually well remembered.
~Louis Dudek

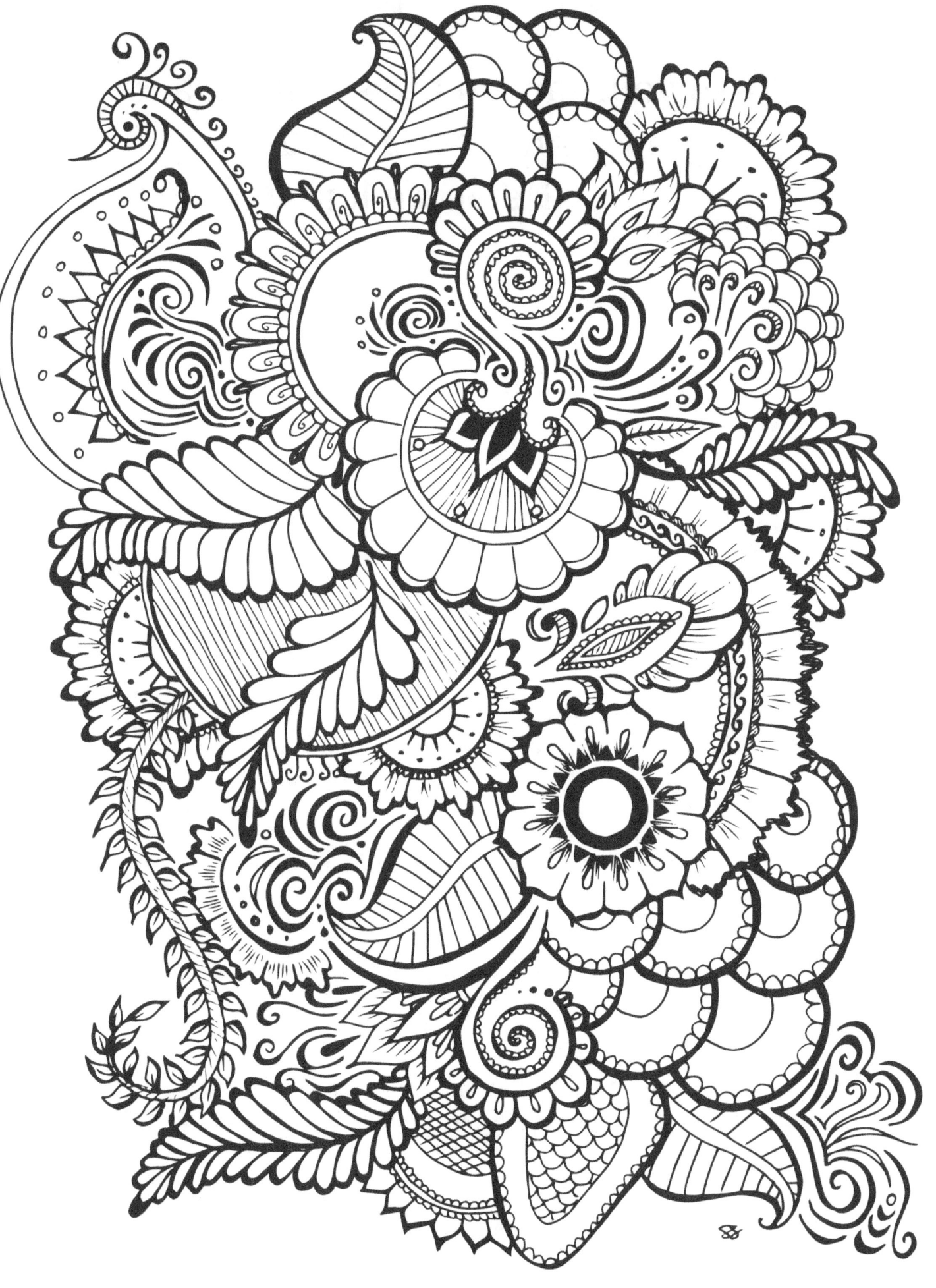

Keep your face to the sunshine and
you cannot see a shadow.
~Helen Keller

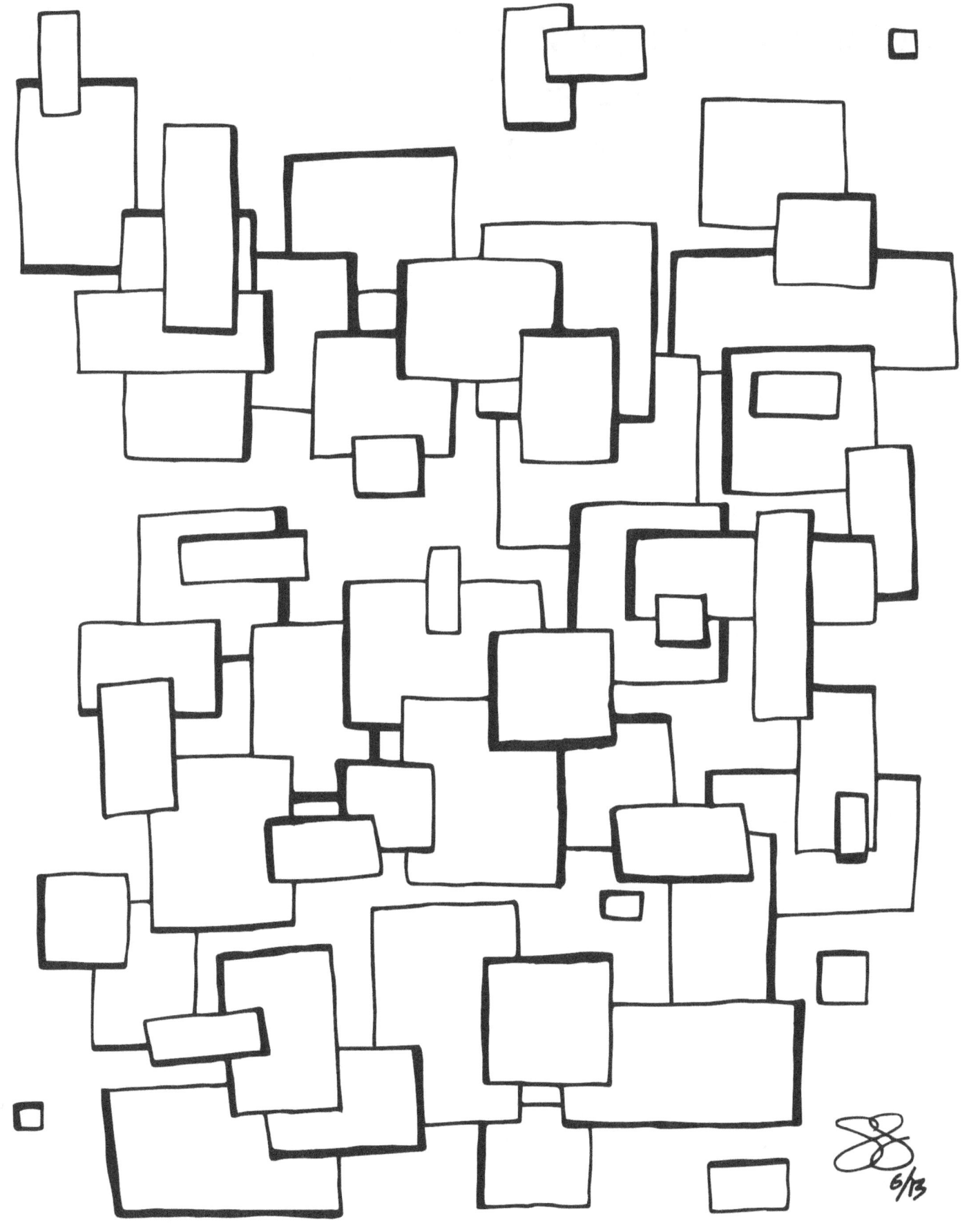

6/13

In order to carry a positive action we must develop
here a positive vision.
~Dalai Lama

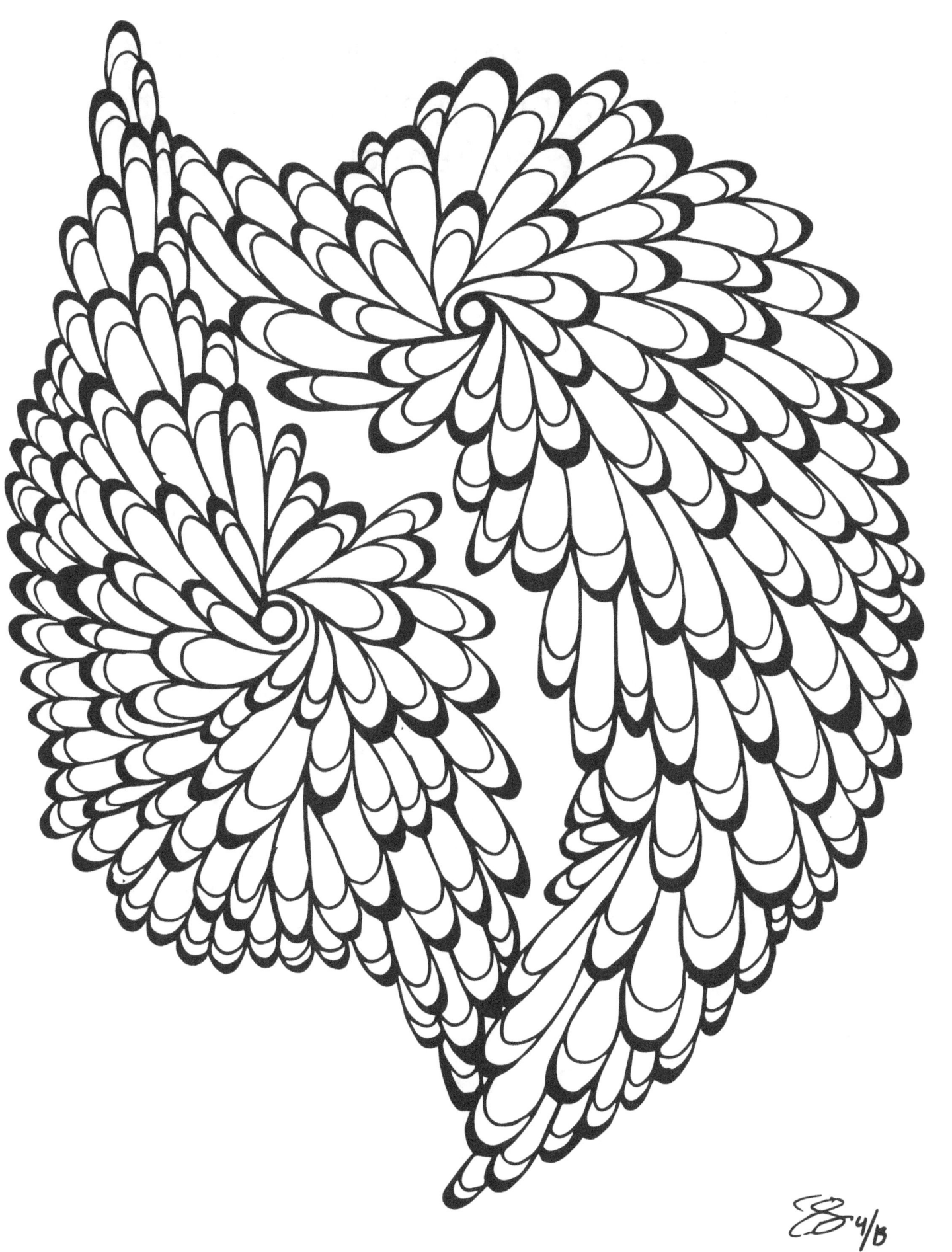

Enthusiasm is excitement with inspiration, motivation, and a pinch of creativity.
~Bo Bennett

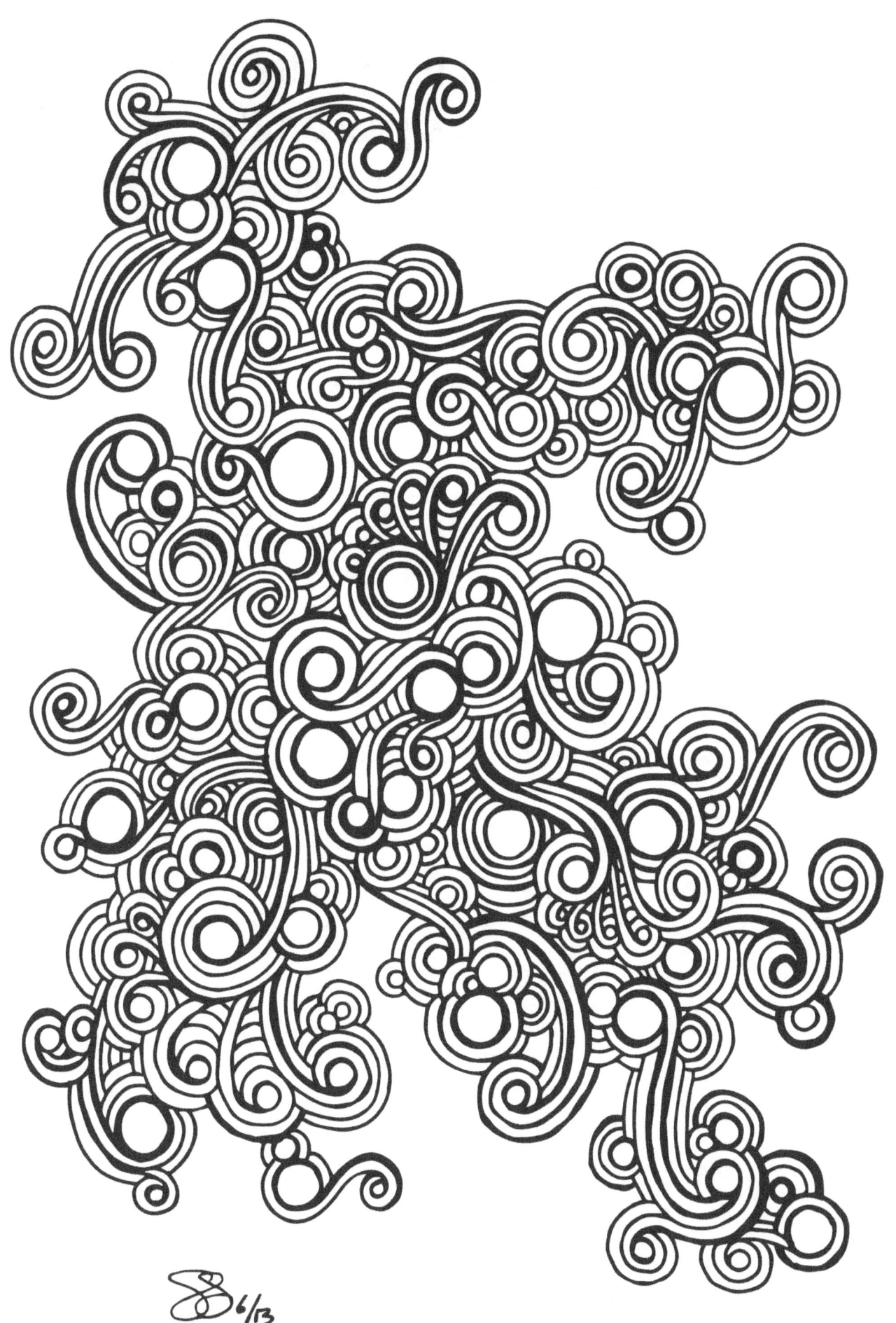

The secret to a happy life is to
accept change gracefully.
~Jimmy Stewart

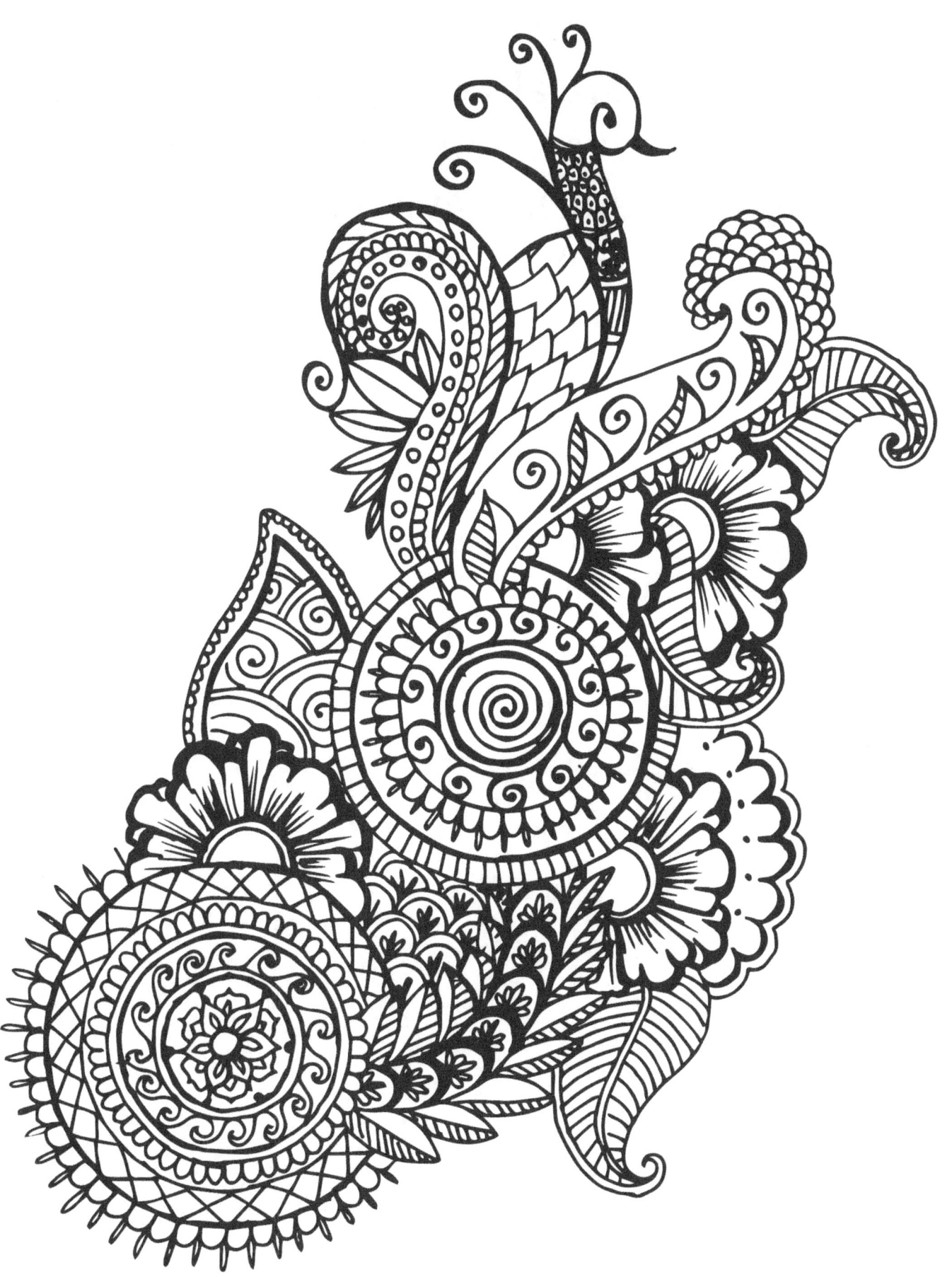

SS 17/12

Some people are always grumbling because roses have thorns; I am thankful thorns have roses.
~Alphonse Karr